Things I Didn't Want to Write
The Poetic Reluctance of
TK Long

In association with In Her Write Mind, LLC

For Shamika and Elaine and the women they were becoming

THINGS I DIDN'T WANT TO WRITE: THE POETIC RELUCTANCE OF TK LONG. Copyright © 2020 by TK Long.

Table of Contents

I Don't Want to Write 1
Bare 2
Nina in Variation 3
Purple Heart 5
Real Love 6
Black Child 7
I Hate U 9
Love Song 10
Burned 13
Let Love Rule 14
The Shit 15
HER (At the Airport) 17
Pieces 18
Graveyard 20
Tools of War 21
Pep Talk 22
Hey, Kalief 23
About the Sky 25
Freedom 26
Safety 27
5 A.M. 28
I Made You a Mixtape 29
For REAL 31
Priceless 32
Paul Revere 33
What Happened to Sandra Bland? 34
Grand Canyon 35
On Writing 36
Shamika 37
Princess Nobody 38
Good Riddance 39

Build 41
Secret of the Sun 42
Staring at Staff Paper 43
Lost One 44
Changed 45
Signs 46
Transplant 47
Running in Place 48
WHOAman 49
Invested 50
Black Man 51
Not Anymore 52
Broken Lines 53
Nothing Compares 2 U 54
No Love 55
Come Closer 56
Unpacking 57
Love 58
Happily, Never After 59
Be Art 60
After Church 61
Not the Girl 63
The Sorry You Didn't Say 64
'Round Midnight 65
Ashes to Ashes: The Case for Cremation 66
Sentimental Mood 67
Zora 68
Forget Me Lots 69
Be Free 70
The Beautiful Struggle 71

Functional 72
Up 73
Black People 74
The Other Woman 76
Ms. Cellophane 77
Don't Give Up 78
Liquidity 79
Little One 80
STILL the Wrong Alice 81
Mirror 82
Apparition 84
He Was Music 85
rEVOLution 87
How to Love 88
Nope 89
Dazed & Confused (Thinking In My Garage) 90
Anachronistic 91
Home 92
Black 93
Lear 94

I Don't Want to Write

Sometimes I sit and think about you.

I don't speak.

I don't write anything down.

I just let you play inside my mind.

I let you tickle the hypotheses of us and

Caress our could be.

I can feel your breath all over my theories.

You give my "just waits" the sweetest kisses.

There are times that I don't want to write about you.

Sometimes I just want you…here.

TK

Bare

I am most beautiful when I let go.

During the times I throw up my hands

And let it all fall, I glow.

The heaviness hits the ground and shatters.

Shards fly

But I relish in the fact that

They are down there, and I am up here.

No inhibitions cloak my joy.

No indifference clouds my peace.

No intolerance veils my being.

I am most perfect

When I am laid bare.

TK

Nina In Variation

I am Nina in variation.
I am what suits you.

In the times you are at war,
I am the Simone sort-
A beautiful revolutionary
Colored with complexity.
I'm never afraid to speak my mind
Because I have the power to make
Whatever I say sound like music.
If I lash out at you, it is only because
Of my passion and the things
We are both still working to understand about me.
I'm just a soul whose intentions are good.
Love me anyway.
You won't regret it.

When you want peace,
I am of the Mosley mindset.
I am your muse when you don't
Even know you need one.
I am that silent whisper that pushes past
Your manhood and exposes you.
I mean, the *real* you.
With me, there is no on-stage persona
Hidden behind the paint of pretty words.
I am the last to make love to you
But the first to strip you bare.
I let you be the blues in my left thigh
Knowing you will crave the funk in my right.
When you meet yourself through me,
But still don't understand,
Love me anyway.
You won't regret it.

I am steel.
I am that thing you hold in your hands
That makes you realize the power
Of life and death.

I give you the rush of knowing
You have the strength to kill
But when the sun catches me just right,
You no longer want to.
The curves of my body gleam brightly
And leave you entranced.
You ponder the ingenuity it took to create me.
I'm heavy in your hands.
But your heart and mind are lighter
Knowing that I am here if you ever need me.
When others misuse me
And diminish my beauty,
Love me anyway.
You won't regret it.

I exist in many forms
But always perfectly.
I am a magnificent masterpiece.
I am all you will ever need.

TK

Purple Heart

There's a war going on inside of you.

I want nothing more than to help you wage it.

I want to charge into battle with you

And join in on your battle cry.

I want to feel the metal of the enemy's sword.

I want to be able to bleed for you.

You are so battered already.

I want to be the one you can lean on

And limp away with, bearing a victorious smile.

I would cheer loudest when they pin on your medal

And give you a few badges of my own.

You are the bravest soldier I know.

I would be honored to fight beside you.

But I am ill-equipped and I can't come with you.

With my deepest regret, I must let you go alone.

But with outstretched arms,

I will be waiting here when you make it home.

TK

Real Love

Real Love is on life support.

It took a nasty fall from its pedestal,

Which is ironic because

PEOPLE used to fall into IT.

It is lying in a hospital that is busy with people

Running crazy to breathe life into everything that doesn't matter.

Fame gets the antibiotics Real Love needs.

The splints are put on Skin Deep Beauty.

Money gets the bandages.

Sex gets the sutures.

Casts go on Vicious Cycles to hold in their vitality.

Gurneys race down the halls ushering in new insignificant patients.

Tears are shed at their bedsides and people stop at nothing

To keep them all alive.

But Real Love gets no visitors.

It lies alone, busted and bruised,

Ignored,

Clinging to life.

TK

Black Child

Black Child, I want you to invite you to love yourself.

I mean, I'm going to.

So, you might as well join me.

I'm going to adore the way your skin is that shade of brown

That fits perfectly between your mama's and your daddy's.

It's almost like they waited for years for you to come along

And fill that empty bit of canvas that already held a pretty picture.

I'm going to love the kinks and coils of your hair

And how some days, it just doesn't know the meaning of gravity.

I'm going to love watching wiry limbs that don't know what

To do with themselves suddenly become Double Dutch acrobats.

I'm going to love the smiles that spread across your thick lips

As Miss Mary Mack and her silver buttons are given life

With the rhythm from your hands.

I'm going to love you on makeshift basketball courts

Where your passion for the game is the reason you know

That if you cuss about it a little, ain't nobody gon' tell.

I'm going to love you when you're on the corner.

I know you don't skip school because you're dumb.

It is just taking you a while to learn that all easy money ain't good money.

When you sell your body, I know you only do it because

No one has ever truly shown you what you're worth.

If you only knew, you would know that any price is beneath you.

I'm going to love you from the halls of high school to Harvard.

Some think you won't make it there, but I believe in you.

I already know why I love you and why I always will.

In a world that gives you every reason to hate yourself, love is what you need most.

And it might as well start with you and me.

TK

I Hate U

I have never hated you more than

I do for the way you made me love you

Five minutes ago.

Don't get me wrong.

I fall for you every day

But the falling should stop once I decide to be angry.

I really thought I was ready this time.

I had that fold-my-arms-and-turn-my-head-

Don't-laugh-at-any-of-his-jokes-or-caress-his-cheek-

Let-alone-kiss-him

Act down to a science.

Then you went and said something sweet and wrecked the whole thing.

Now I'm sitting here hating you but

With a bigger problem on my hands

Because I can't decide if I hate myself

More than I hate you because I fell for

Your sweet shit when I was supposed to be cool.

I'm really not sure you're worth

This kind of trouble.

I'm enjoying this radio silence though.

I needed this time alone with

My thoughts.

Let me enjoy them while I can.

Pretty soon that phone will ring.

And I will have to start hating you

All over again.

TK

Love Song

I'm doing something different this time.

This time, I'm writing a love song for myself.

I'm saving the most beautiful notes I have ever heard for ME.

There are some in there that will make me cry.

But I will love and embrace myself afterward and

All will be well.

I don't have to worry about sticking to a format or

Be concerned that it is too long for listening.

With this song, the longer the better.

The instruments will move me,

But the lyrics hold the power.

These are all the things I will say to myself on

The days I feel low.

These words will be putty for all the cracks in my heart.

Some cracks, I will admit are self-inflicted.

They come from loving too hard when others love too little.

But I won't feel bad for that.

Only healing will matter once the music starts.

There will be a special verse for days like this

When my mind lingers on someone who has made me a mere afterthought.

You know.

When I have loved only to have it

Thrown back in my face.

He may have mattered to me for years.

But I will hum my tune all day and he won't matter by morning.

There will be a verse for friends.

I will sing the love of those who are devout and

Give those who are not their long-awaited benediction.

I will ask that they go with God because they

Are no longer invited to go with me.

My family will get a verse too.

As plentiful as we are,

I am one of a kind.

I have been told I have a face similar to my mother's

And a demeanor similar to my brother's

But my spirit is all my own.

I will sing praises to only those who respect that.

The longest verse will be for me.

That dreamer,

That wild hearted lover,

That sensitive soul that has been hardened by time,

That girl who is angry at the world often but

Rarely admits it because she has been told it is wrong

That girl who is sick of being told what is wrong

Or that *she* is wrong

That girl who stands naked in the mirror with

Dents and dimples and a belly bigger than it was a decade ago

And searches for a reason to love herself,

That girl who is tired but may never show it,

That girl who cries herself to sleep sometimes

But can make you wonder if she ever feels sad at all,

That broken girl who still has some honest smiles left,

That girl who is most beautiful when she loves freely

And is attempting to trust enough to do so again,

That girl who is not perfect but is worth every

Second invested in her,

That girl who is becoming.

My verse is one I will probably play on a loop.

The truth is, I may be perfecting it for the rest of my life.

I will be working on my love song to myself for a while

But that won't stop me from singing it anyway.

After all, practice makes perfect.

I have to get this right though.

From now on,

It is the only song I will ever sing.

TK

Burned

I'm not sure what you're looking for in my eyes.
But you won't find the fire I used to have.
That was snuffed out when you didn't love me.
You got most of it the first time.
But when I was foolish enough to love you again,
The rest died.
I would like to say that it left my humanity unscathed.
But that's a lie.
It scorched my sensitivity and
Bore holes through my joy.
It spread to my Give-A-Shit and
Melted off its face.
It was useless after that so I decided to throw it out.
My trust was permanently damaged too
After my own raging wildfire ran free.
After your wrath, you couldn't possibly think
I'd be the same.
I should have believed you wanted to be better for me
But I always knew the truth.
My spirit has had its trial by fire.
Please look away so that I can save
What little of me is not yet ash.
.

TK

Let Love Rule

I hope love happens to you.

I mean that scary, crazy, don't-know-what-to-do kind of love.

In the middle of the night, I want you to lie there

Awake and smiling like a fool.

At the times your "one" is not with you,

I want you to feel lost and empty.

When they tell you a joke,

I want those deep belly laughs for you—

The ones that grow from seeds planted in your soul and

Push past the darkness.

When they tell you their secrets,

I want you to be able to see the doors open and

I want you to run wild as you explore what is behind them all.

When they tell you they don't love you anymore,

I want you to be broken and cry until you're exhausted.

When they beg your forgiveness and tell you they don't mean it,

I want you to breathe that sigh of relief and

Fall into their arms.

I want you so consumed with emotion that you can't breathe.

I wish for love to rule you.

TK

The Shit

Today, I realized that I am the shit.

It took a little time.

Last night, I laid down

With the weight of the world on my mind.

But I met myself in my subconscious

While I was asleep.

I forced myself to look at myself and to really dig deep.

My heart was heavier than my eyes and I was a bit of a mess.

But I woke up happy and free today and feeling my absolute best.

I looked at my heart

And realized it was still kind.

Despite all it has seen,

There is love left inside.

I thought about how my mind works

And the corners it bends.

I thought about what I do with my gifts and all the hearts

I hope to mend.

I thought about my friends,

Even though these days, they are few.

I'm blessed that such beautiful people

Stuck around to help me through.

I thought of those who hurt me and

All the pain I thought would last.

I thought about the courage it took to

Leave them all in the past.

I fixed my breaking heart

And checked my emotions at today's door.

What had my heart so heavy

Really doesn't matter anymore.

We all have those rough days

Where nothing seems to go our way.

But today, I feel like I'm the shit.

And I hope tomorrow is your day.

TK

HER (At the Airport)

At first, I just liked her boots. But that was before I saw her—large eyes of an icy blue shade and dark brown skin. She was beautiful. Her brown plaid scarf was less for the Florida sun than for the cold that sometimes happens when you fly the friendly skies. Her black leggings and long-sleeved top were probably chosen for the same reason. Then there were the boots, of course. Her face was adorned by a gold nose ring and matching earrings that dangled and danced when she turned her head. Her dark hair, all but for the edges, hid under a brown hijab that contrasted with her scarf.

"Zone 1!" A voice blared over the PA.

As people passed by, she nervously touched her head. Her icy blue eyes darted around to see what others might have been on her. She played with the ends of her hijab and toyed with the idea of removing it. Her eyes fell on a man who stared at her unyieldingly. Slowly she turned away but glanced over her shoulder to see if he was still watching. He was. What was he thinking? Did her cinnamon complexion make her a threat? Was he wondering how *her* people could have eyes *that* color? Did she look "American enough"? She pulled the end of her hijab free and large, black curls fell upon her shoulders. At first the man still stared. But finally, he looked away. Nervously, she tucked her hair behind her ear and sipped her coffee. She looked defeated. My heart broke for her. I didn't know her destination. But I hoped it was one that was as beautiful as she was.

TK

Pieces

I admit it.

I'm broken.

I have spent all these years trying to look pretty

And polished for you but

It is senseless because I am the one who loses.

Your mind typically runs at one speed

While mine sprints randomly.

I have a hard time keeping pace

Yet I still added Pleasing You as more competition.

You have suggested that I find someone to talk to

When the one I want to talk to most is you.

You have robbed yourself of the

Majesty of me.

It is you who misunderstands

The world.

You see, the world is in the hands of people like me.

Every other day, we are standing out on the ledges

Of the universe.

We bravely feel the wind in our faces without

Knowing if it will burn us or chill us to the bone.

We humble ourselves and imagine a world without us.

We either feel deeply or not at all

But we usually feel out loud.

We have spoken to the flowers enough to know

How they feel when people like you ignore their beauty.

We have seen the world through enough tears

To know how beautiful it is when we have cloudless days.

We have found more of ourselves in heaps upon the floor

Than you have as you travel the globe.

It is true that I have always identified with broken things.

But now I make no apologies for being one of them.

I am fragmented and living freely.

Maybe someday, you will be worthy of all of my

Beautiful pieces.

TK

Graveyard

Where does love go to die?

Maybe if I run fast enough, I can catch it before its last breath.

Then maybe for just a second, I can have

That beautiful dream I used to have and hold it in my hands

Even if only a moment.

For once, I won't have to try to recreate that feeling I had while I slumbered-

That feeling that for once, I am the only one who

Matters to someone—

Like maybe he isn't looking past me for the next girl who

Might be prettier, or taller, or thinner—

That feeling that there is actually hope for me and that I won't

Always be alone.

If I can find this amazing, amorous, apocalyptic place,

I can find a spark of that joy that has refused to die before I

Have a chance to see it.

Maybe if I run fast enough,

Love won't die before I do.

TK

Tools of War

This is not a pen and paper.

This is an arsenal.

It is what I take into war with me every day.

When no one else understands,

It is what identifies with me.

On the days anger and frustration take hold,

It is what gives me peace.

When I want to say words I will regret,

It is what helps me bite my tongue.

When I hurt from the bombs thrown at me,

It is what helps me blink back tears and keep fighting.

It helps me absorb the shocks of gut punches

This cold world throws my way.

When I am under attack,

It is my grenade.

When I am cut open and bleeding out,

It cleans and heals all wounds.

When I am the only soldier left on the field,

It multiplies and becomes a mighty and victorious battalion.

On the days I feel I won't make it home,

It is my map.

It is my weapon of choice.

I'm not sure what you're bringing into battle.

But I'm ready whenever you are.

TK

Pep Talk

Baby Girl, your lungs ain't broken.

You are just too smart to breathe in the bullshit.

They're mosquitoes.

They suck the life out of all that is beautiful.

But you, Firefly, just want to light up the world.

It's funny how in your corner of the world—

Where the colors sound loudest and the

Feelings taste sweetest, you inhale and exhale just fine.

You never have to worry about dark skies or dark nights

Because you make it all much brighter.

Just know that when you're feeling that weight

Sitting in the center of your chest, you are not broken.

Hold your breath and keep dreaming.

You are wise not to become what you behold.

TK

Hey, Kalief

Hey, Kalief.

You don't know it. But you are my brother.

Seriously.

I have one at home just like you.

He's a gentle soul who can change the world.

But he so happens to have dark skin.

What he does or doesn't do never matters.

As long as he does or doesn't do it while

Wearing that dark skin,

There is no difference between his guilt and innocence.

At any given time, he can be beaten for wearing it.

He didn't go to solitary the way you did.

But he is isolated within the dirty walls of his trauma too.

He will always, in some way, be treated like that thing

That is adjacent to human.

He, too, finds himself trapped amongst groups

With which he doesn't belong.

Like you, he is accused of stealing something but

What they are saying he took are the things that should

Have been given to him anyway.

He should have had basic human decency handed to him on a platter

But again, because of the skin he wears, it is rationed.

He is allowed to exist but there is little respect for the space he occupies.

Those who feel they granted that space to him can come in

When they want and do what they want.

After all, they aren't the ones who wear the dark skin that

Seems to be a curse.

Kalief, I pray that unlike you, my brother never has a May 15, 2010.

With everything I have in me, I want to protect him.

But you see, I wear the dark skin too.

I am slightly more agile in mine because the aggression they assume

From me is not as strong as his.

When I don't smile, they might suspect anger.

But if he doesn't, he could end up in cuffs or worse.

I couldn't save you, Kalief.

For that I'm sorry.

And I know it sounds selfish to say that I don't want to

Cry the same tears your sister did.

But it would be a lie to say that wasn't my goal.

I failed you, Kalief.

But I am hoping and praying that I don't fail him too.

TK

About the Sky

I love the sky.

I admire her quick sense of get-your-shit-togetherness

After a storm.

Within an instant, she can see past her troubles.

She wipes all the clouds from her face and

Dashes on some sunshine.

She doesn't hold in her anger either.

She lets her thunder roar loudly

So that we all know when something isn't right.

She uses her tears for whatever she wants.

She can either destroy or cultivate what is beneath her.

If she's feeling extra fancy,

She lays on some lightning and shows off a little.

If she just wants things to stand still for a while,

She shakes on some snow and stops them in their tracks.

She can bring about the worst

But when she bats her bright beautiful blues,

All is always forgiven.

She's bold.

She's powerful and she is wholly herself.

I want to be just like her.

TK

Freedom

To be able to give yourself to someone only when you choose—
And not those borrowed parts you had to sneak to pluck because you
Thought they looked pretty growing in your neighbor's yard
But now that they are planted in yours, they don't grow the same because your soil is different
No
I'm not talking about those parts at all
I'm talking about the parts of you that are innate
The parts that always grew within you organically
And never made room for the borrowed shit because it would just die there anyway
The parts you lived and thrived on from birth because they and you have always been enough
The parts of you that were healthy and vibrant because they were rested and whole
And not exhausted from searching for damns to give about everything
The parts of you that are content with celebrating yourself the way you see fit
And never being swayed by the thoughts of the parties you SHOULD be throwing
The parts of you that don't fear the tears but welcome them because
They nourish that good, organic, enough, healthy vibrant content shit
You should be focused on anyway
To be able to decide NOT to give yourself to someone when you don't choose
To say "I'm keeping these parts for me"—
That's freedom.

TK

Safety

Come here, My Love.
The day is showing on your face.
When you're out there fighting,
Your armor is always expected to be strong
So, no one ever notices the cracks.
You have held it up for years so everyone assumes
The weight doesn't bother you.
But I can see it.
You're tired from having to fight against the gale force winds
That charge toward you.
Your stature is a bit misleading because you
Tower over much of the world but I know
That after being told for so long that you have no place in this world,
You only seek to disprove the theories.
Others don't know that you're breaking though.
To them, you are still intimidating,
That ominous thing that seeks to destroy what they have gained.
But I can see it.
All you want, even if just for a moment, is to be that version
Of you that everyone has forgotten.
You want to be surrounded by your favorite things,
To hurt without explanation,
To laugh without suspicion,
To cry without judgement
To love without fear.
To be protected.
Rest here.
You are safe with me.

TK

5 a.m.

Give yourself to me at 5 a.m.

I want those moments between dreams and coherence.

I want that second you open your eyes to greet the world.

I want the time before your mind forms

Its first thought of the day.

I want to be there when you start to happen.

At 5 a.m., you would keep nothing from me.

The tools you would need to do so

Will not have stretched their legs yet.

When you roll over and look at me,

I can watch your eyes adjust to my light

As you get to know me again.

When I touch you at 5 a.m.

There is no time for engineered dirty thoughts to cross your mind.

At 5 a.m., you *feel*, purely and exclusively.

I have seen 5 a.m. many times over but now I know

That I want to see all of mine with you.

TK

I Made You A Mixtape

I made you a mixtape of everything I have ever felt

And left it on your doorstep today.

I started with "The Day We Met" and the tune is kind of sweet.

It starts off slow and in certain places, it's cute and all over the place.

After that comes "That First Phone Conversation".

Be patient with that one because it's long and probing.

"Our First Date" comes next.

It's a song filled with questions

But "I wonder if he wants to do this again as much as I do"

Is the best part.

"That Time We Took That Road Trip" and "When You Met My Friends" are

Happy, peppy tunes that will make your heart bounce a bit.

"The Day I Knew I Loved You" is deep and it lingers with every note.

It will start at your head and tell you everything glorious about yourself.

At the end, it fills the space so much that you will feel it stand next to you like flesh and blood.

"Pictures on The Wall" and "Waking Up to You"

Celebrate you even more and they may make you blush.

"Skin to Skin" will make the places you blush burn with pure passion.

"Late Hours at Work" and "No Time For Each Other" cool that off though.

"Growing Apart" is sad and will give you that feeling you get when you are falling

But rather than ever putting you out of your misery and

Letting you hit the ground,

It just repeats itself a few times.

"Why Don't You Love Me Anymore?" hurts because it is a song with no resolution.

The chords are unfinished and the melody changes constantly like it is frantic and

Has no clue what to do.

You can hear the death of us in the song but if you are anything like me,

You will keep listening and hoping you can fix it.

"What Does She Have That I Don't?" is awful because the lyrics will make you

Look at all the things that were once glorious

And find their defects.

"Saying Goodbye" is the worst because I am still not okay with the way that one sounds.

The notes, the lyrics, the cadence—everything about that one is off.

I left the mixtape for you.

You may just skip to the songs you like.

Then again, you may not listen at all.

In the end, you never did.

TK

For REAL

When I fall in love—I mean fall in love for REAL—the feeling is going to need to be close to the one I get from music. When my heart is broken, I need to know that I don't hurt by myself. I need to laugh and sing to the tops of my lungs even when I don't know the words. I want to dance when I'm tired and nod my head to a beat created just for me.

It needs to encourage me like The Staple Singers, tell my truth like PJ Morton, teach me like Donny Hathaway, speak to me like Miles Davis, move me like Floetry, understand me like John Legend, give me chills like Sam Cooke, make me a bit gutsy like Big K.R.I.T., put me together like Prince and show my greatness off like James Brown and Jill Scott.

Yeah. When I fall in love—I mean fall in love for REAL—the melody is going to have to move through me. Otherwise, I'm just not doing it.

TK

Priceless

Are you expecting me to ask for the moon?

Are you dreading standing before a mighty merchant with

Only everything you have and feeling inadequate when you still can't afford it?

Do you fear seeing disappointment on my face

When I find out I will just have to watch it shine from a distance?

Are you thinking that pretty soon, I'll want

One of those pyramids I admire so much?

Do you think I will see you as less of a man when you tell me

I will just have to be content seeing them between pages?

Do you think I'll ask for the world?

Do you think I'll think you don't love me when you tell me

You came up short and couldn't haggle for me?

You really do have it all wrong.

All I want is that honesty your face used to carry

When you said you loved me.

I want the heaviness of your mind and that feather-light feeling

Of hearing you laugh.

I want that peaceful babbling just before you fall asleep.

I want the gentle rise and fall of your chest as you dream.

I want the sweetness of your celebrations and the

Stark bitterness of the lessons you learn.

It is not humanly possible to put a price on those.

You are the most valuable currency I know.

TK

Paul Revere

Fuck you and the horse your rode in on.
You decided to breeze through my life and
Wreck everything in the process.
I carried a torch for you and I trusted you to hold the flame
But I never thought you would use it to burn me.
It's easy at this point for you to ride by when you see me breaking
Because you never got off that horse in the first place.
Sure, you would bend down to kiss me
And hoist me up to defile me.
But you never brought yourself down to common ground
With me
When I said, "I love you", it must have sounded different by the
Time it reached you up there.
They sounded like divine words to me because you said
It back from such an altitude.
When I said I missed you, it was easy for you
Because you could look down from where you were and
Catch a glimpse of me
So, you never missed me at all
You're okay with the fire you set and all the fortresses
You have leveled within me
Because, after all, you have that damn horse
So, keep riding
Pretend to care and leave behind your crocodile tears.
As you ride off into the sunset
I will pretend I would be sad if that same sun
Burns you along your way.

TK

What Happened to Sandra Bland?

What are you trying to tell me? Your eyes keep haunting me as though you really do want me to know what happened to you. Unfortunately, you can't part your lips. Are you wanting me to know that they took you from us and treated you like some marionette that they dressed, posed and pulled strings on so that you told the story they saw fit? The fact that the keen, sculpted point you had to your nose is completely gone, your skin that was once a lot like mine now shows ominous blotches and your crown and glory falls backwards as though caught in the wind tells me something isn't right. As you lie upon that floor knowing that your regal frame of 6 feet did not perish from only 5, your spirit practically screams "Foul play!" I know firsthand that depression can be fought with life and I know you knew that too. It's true. You had your flaws. We all do. You knew so much about our people's struggles so I had hopes that soon you would be able to see the light on the struggles of ALL of us. Because you also knew your rights and fought for them, you had to be the example. Dear martyr, the heads of the guilty hit their pillows but tears of sorrow hit mine. Strong-willed and opinionated, I know you would tell me what happened if you could. But now you never will.

TK

Grand Canyon

I can't close the chasm.
Instead, the only thing I can do is stare at you across this great divide.
I can see you self-destructing from where I'm sitting.
You aren't recovering from your injuries very well.
You are mistaken to think that just because you
Can't see my scars that I no longer have any.
It was a long time ago that I clawed my way out of the trench
But some wounds just don't heal.
My love legs are still fractured but all these years,
I have been able to tone down my limp.
So, instead of thinking I'm hurting,
You think I'm just being cool about it.
It's not that "cool" that keeps me from mentioning it.
The truth is, I'm hoarse from screaming at you
In a language you don't understand anymore.
I don't even have the peace of a babbling stream below
To count on.
Instead, I pass the time watching the migrations of
Buzzards overhead that wait to eat your dead things as soon as you let them go.
But you hold on to your dead things.
You hold them much tighter than you ever held me.
You hold them because they are familiar.
When you need a reason to blame someone else,
They provide.
They keep you empty and allow you to fill yourself
With the things that will keep you wanting.
Your wanting makes you feel alive.
It gives you purpose.
While you grip your dead things, your eyes are fixed on me.
Since I can't speak to you,
I try to send you pieces of my heart.
But even they don't reach anymore.
They get about halfway to you then they run out of steam
And fall to their deaths.
Rather than run out of pieces to send you,
I stay still and hope your curiosity about the pieces you've missed
Will get the best of you.
I hope you will let go of those things that will never again have a pulse
And climb down to look for them.
I hope that this fissure, this break,
This gaping hole we love across
Can someday make a wonder of itself.

TK

On Writing

I like to stand on the edge of myself when I write. I like to step outside and stare back at every emotion I could ever imagine. It is the only time I can look at all of me at once. It is that standing naked in front of the ultimate mirror of truth that frees me. When I look at my fears, I don't always have to look for the ways to overcome them. In those moments, I really don't have to be heroic. I can hurt and never have to explain why. I can cry without the embarrassment of anyone seeing my face when I do it. I can be angry. I can yell on the page and still get a second chance to rationally approach a situation. It seems like when I am writing, I always seem to fall in love the right way. If it's mutual, I grow. If not, I learn. When I'm writing, that special person always touches me just the way I need them to and they always allow me to touch them the way that every part of me desires. I am never left wanting. I get to love and live without complication. And so, I write.

TK

Shamika

God dedicated The Moon to you that night.
He must have because we had never seen it that way before.
He gave it a new red dress to wear once it took off
The black one it wore to that party a few years back.
It got all fancy for us.
He must have known it was the last time I would see you.
He knew it was the last time you would smile at me
And the last time I would hear your voice.
You and I had to see The Moon put on her new dress
Before you left.
You didn't have much energy for dancing but
She knew that She still had to get dressed for you.
You're special, My Love.
You always have been.
You couldn't stay for the party and
I was a bit too sad to dance without you.
But it is good to know that you made it to the other party that
God threw in your honor.
You did get a chance to rest on your journey to meet Him.
He healed your pain along the way and took away all your worry.
When you arrived, He had your dancing shoes laid out for you
And a dress much brighter than the one He had given The Moon.
Now you have energy to dance for days.
And Aunt Elaine has been waiting to show you some joyous moves.
The Moon and her dress are no match for you.
God dedicated the moon to you that night.
He knew that you and She were majesty like none had ever seen.

TK

(January 20, 2019. The night of the Super Wolf Blood Moon and our last time together on Earth.)

Princess Nobody

I should have known I couldn't be Cinderella.

They don't make glass slippers big enough for these feet.

Just like the rest of me, they are too big,

Too much and all over the place.

These hands aren't made for rings.

Bright symbols of love just don't belong here.

There are far too many dreams in this head for a crown to fit.

And I don't have a face that says any of them will come true.

I'm not Snow White either-

Even if any fruit I am given does have the intent to poison me.

Yes, someday my prince will come.

But he will wave to me, thank me for clearing his path

And ride on to meet the fairest in the land.

Like Belle, I have found my beast,

But it isn't me that he is looking to transform for.

He is looking for the rose with the enchanted petals,

Not the one with the noticeable thorns.

So, I will stay here, high up in this tower,

Longing for the happy ending not meant for me.

TK

Good Riddance

Girl, thank you for taking him off my hands!

Now he can be *your* sorry excuse for a man.

Honestly, he's useless.

It took me this long to see.

But I'm sure he told you he was God's gift to me.

Well, he didn't come in a pretty package.

He wasn't tied with a bow.

He left me patting my pockets and asking,

"Where'd that gift receipt go?"

I wanted to return him.

A prize, he is not.

He was already in the cart but thanks for meeting me in the parking lot.

I was looking for a man who was ready, willing and able.

But instead, I took home petty, weak and emotionally unstable.

Maybe you will be the girl he brags on and always flaunts.

But I hope he doesn't switch gears on you the moment you don't

Do what he wants.

If you pick him up when he is down and help him better himself,

I hope he isn't using your light to help him love someone else.

When you call him out for being radio silent for days at a time,

I hope he doesn't look at you like you have lost your mind.

When all you have ever wanted was to build a family,

I hope he doesn't avoid the subject the way he did with me.

When you just want to spend every night with him,

I hope you don't end up wondering just where the hell he's been.

My shackles are off.

I'm free!

This is the end of my sentence.

You may say "He's mine now".

But Sweetie, I just say "Good riddance".

TK

Build

I want that "I've never seen it. But I hear it's beautiful"
Kind of relationship with you.
No, really. Those are the conversations I want to have.
I want us to talk about all the things we have been told
Were wondrous and dream of seeing them together.
I'm talking about the rain in Spain,
The peaks of the pyramids and the lights of The Eiffel Tower.
But after we make that list,
I want us to take those steps to creating a future.
I want us to be able to forget about all the old things
That didn't allow us to witness wonders.
I want to not even be able to see the
Old shanties of shame for all the new
Pitched roofs of positivity we have put up.
I want us both to know that not living in nirvana now
Doesn't mean we can never make it.
We have all the materials we need.
So, let's just build our Beautiful.

TK

Secret of the Sun

The sun told me a secret today.

She finally admitted there actually is

Something special she does when she shines on you.

She does this thing where she reaches inside

Of you and pulls everything I love to the surface.

She brings the things I'm learning

To love too.

She positions them at different angles

And lets me see them all in new light.

She never admitted it before

Because she wasn't sure how I would feel

About her giving you special treatment.

But right now,

I'm looking at all of you in the light.

And I'm not mad at all.

TK

Staring at Staff Paper

I can only hope to someday be as important as a single note of music. It carries the beauty of being a part of an arrangement or being everything and nothing on its own. It meets with friends to build movements to propel life forward or stands alone and repeats itself and causes life to stand still. It is lonely, but it is also the best company kept. A single music note understands that when you don't belong anywhere, you can thrive everywhere. When she is sad, she is beautiful. When she is happy, she is radiant. When she stands alone, she is strong. When she is vulnerable, it is accepted and the undying support makes her strong again. She is imperfect. She is everything.

TK

Lost One

I am Success's displaced child.

I know the comfort of her embrace because

I was born to be hers.

But our home is war torn.

Over the years, bombs have flown and

Fires of failure and fear have separated us.

The debris of doubt blocks our path.

But I will keep crying out.

A mother never forgets her child's voice.

I will keep fighting.

I will find my way home to her.

TK

Changed

It's too late.
We've loved and now we can't turn back.
We will never again be those same
People we used to be.
Suddenly, we're so deep that we fall
Into ourselves sometimes.
We can formulate thoughts but they
Get wrapped around emotions and
Sometimes don't make it out.
We have never known the
Joyful fear we are about to enter into
Because there is only one place it exists.
We entered the realm when our hearts
Were opened and the portal sealed up behind us.
I'm sure there is a science to learning
To live differently.
We now have to add watching and trusting
To our behavior.
We have become lovers.
And never again can we be anything else.

TK

Signs

Something in the wind says we're not going to make it.

Maybe it's the way it blew eerily over me this morning

And made me think of jackets

Rather than having your arms to hold me close.

The sun came in on the conversation and was sweet enough to

Replace the wind but made me think of being in

A barren desert

Rather than the many articles of clothing I could remove before

Getting next to you.

I think the trees know something too because they don't sway freely

In the breeze but teeter rapidly in indecision.

The clouds are aware, I know, because they float away from me

As if to flee to someone with better luck.

The grass can't fool me either.

I know it has intentionally become less bountiful beneath my feet

And left me with only a hard ground to contend with.

Water doesn't flow the same way.

Its ripples make not exclamation points but

Sad eyes that apologize with every blink.

Hills no longer rise to meet me but wave farewell at a distance.

Rainbows don't say hello but tuck their heads behind the clouds.

The babbling brook says nothing but leaves an uncomfortable silence.

Raindrops frantically fall on my face to save me the embarrassment my of tears.

The lightning and the thunder cease because they pity me.

You and I aren't meant to be.

And all of the earth knows it.

TK

Transplant

Let's trade hearts for a second.

Since you seem so convinced that this one will heal,

Everything should be fine, right?

You keep telling me it won't always be broken,

So, the pain you inherit should be temporary.

I've already done the hard part and

And bore the fresh breaks and bleeding.

The only thing you have to do is

Hold still so the pieces don't go where they shouldn't.

You tell me everything will be fine

But I feel like it's the end.

So, if I put my broken heart with your brain that knows everything,

It should all work out.

Right?

If I'm as great as you say I am,

I deserve to be as lighthearted and carefree as you.

Don't I?

I appreciate your sympathy

But what I would really appreciate

Is if you would take over for a while.

If you believe what you say,

It should all be over soon.

TK

Running in Place

You change me.

You make me second guess everything I say and do.

You always make me feel like I am just not SOMETHING enough.

With all the gusto of a foolish schoolgirl,

I have the nerve to pursue you.

You're broken and emotionally unavailable

And the truth is, I would die before the pursuit is a success.

I am in awe of you.

So, I fool myself into thinking that the

Breadcrumb trail of communication you grant me is enough.

Deep down, I know that with you,

I will always be starving.

I will want what you refuse to give as a result of your own

Arrogance and knowing that you are

What I want most.

There will always be that looming feeling

Of inferiority and fatigue of just

Trying to be SOMETHING enough.

But I must keep running.

I have to outrun my desire for you.

That is, if I ever want to save myself.

TK

WHOAman

I have decided that it is time for my revolution.

Here and now,

I'm raising my fist and my voice.

Long silenced by the so-called strength of my counterpart,

I am just about ready to belt out a tune.

Man is called strong while it is I who

Bear the children,

Birth and nurse the children,

Manage the home,

Work harder for less pay and

Navigate emotions about the crumbling world alone

All while putting myself AND my man back together. Several

times, I have been a tree that has fallen in the forest. But

because I feared it waking my children,

I couldn't afford to make a sound.

But enough of that.

I'm slinging my baby onto my hip, taking my briefcase in hand

And planting my own damn forest.

The soil will be rich with my hope and perseverance and

The roots to all my fellow trees will have undying support.

There, we will all stand

Strong

Proud

Unmoving

And more majestic than any man could ever dream.

TK

Invested

You're my new wallet. You are that precious thing I have been given that I am keeping someplace safe. Though I know you're there, every now and then, I check to be sure. If I haven't seen you in a while or you aren't in my line of sight, I begin to retrace my steps. I wonder if I have truly lost you and what I could have done to prevent it. But when you come back, I light up. I am aware that there is a chance you won't be around forever, but I wish for it anyway. You see, shortly after I got you, I placed my remaining hope for love within you. I gave you my last $5. So, in addition to thinking you're nice to look at, I'm invested in you. Rather than have you leave and allow my heart to suffer the pains of bankruptcy, I subconsciously check the pocket nearest to my heart to be sure you are still there. You're my new wallet—the most beautiful thing I have seen in quite some time.

TK

Black Man

I remember you.

I'm not talking about this thuggish version of you

They want everyone to believe in.

I only know your royalty.

I see how you protect the Black Woman and lead your kingdom.

I see how, despite everything, you always keep pushing through.

When you're in danger, the sirens don't sound for you.

But you persist through the fear.

When they say you're not fit to learn,

You rise and teach the masses.

They never expect you to take care of your children,

But you nurture and raise them as kings and queens.

I see the way you love others even at the times

You struggle to love yourself.

I remember you.

And

I appreciate you.

TK

Not Anymore

I used to wish that love would come to find you.

Even though you and I didn't work,

I wanted to believe that deep down you were still good and kind.

I wanted to believe that we would both get our happy ending

Even if we weren't together.

Life pulled no punches when it came to teach you lessons.

Some of which you have grown from,

Others, you are still striving to screw up perfectly.

So much about you has changed

But I still see glimmers of the old you.

I have learned a lot.

I no longer wish for love to come find you.

But now I offer it my apologies.

Now I know that love deserves much better than you.

TK

Broken Lines

I have no clue how to express myself

But I do it anyway.

Instead of "I really like you",

It comes out as the constant "WYD" that probably has you rolling your eyes.

Instead of "Would you like to go out?",

It comes out, "We should hang out sometime".

"Hang out"? Are we thirteen?

Rather than "I miss you" or "I want to see you",

I say, "If you are ever in the area…"

I don't just say "I love you".

I give you some goofy ass "I think you're cool."

I don't even say "I was thinking about you".

You just get a lame "Hey".

And I know you are worth so much more.

I understand you are confused about how I feel.

What's worse is that I know exactly how I feel

But I am holding back.

Who am I saving it for? No one else is worthy.

If I would just grow up a little before I address you,

I can stop doing you these disservices.

Maybe if I just leave you alone and start my growing now,

I may be worthy of you by the time

You even notice that I am missing.

TK

Nothing Compares 2 U

Damn the Mona Lisa.
The Sistine Chapel is a bore.
All the painted things think they are art
Because they've never seen you before.
You're not confined to clay or stuck up on a wall.
You see life.
You see beauty.
You move through us all.
You make Picasso jealous.
Romare Bearden? Who is he?
If anyone wants to see real art,
I'll just show them you, honestly.
I'll show them how you sigh and lay your head upon my chest.
The way you say my name is perfection, nothing less.
I'll show them the way you glance at me
And smile between your words.
I'm sure they'd agree your voice is
The sweetest sound ever heard.
You're much more hypnotizing than Dali.
You pose.
You talk.
You dance.
Nothing else in the history books will ever stand a chance.
MoMa, The Louvre, Uffizi—
They can tour them all if they want to.
They can ooh and ahh until they're tired.
But nothing compares to you.

TK

No Love

I ain't writing about love today.

I don't care how much you want to hear about butterflies

And somebody making you weak in the knees.

You won't get it from me today.

I don't have time to plant flowers

In the barren field that you call your imagination.

Don't expect me to give you the words to say

To the one you feel you can't do without.

If you want an eargasm or that warm feeling in

Your literary loins,

You are out of luck.

You will have to look elsewhere for that poetic pitter patter

And the sonnets that sets your soul ablaze.

Talk to somebody else about love.

'Cause today,

It just ain't on my mind.

TK

Come Closer

Come a little closer

And let me taste your soul.

Let me lick along the lines of

Your intellect and taste what nourishment it yields.

Allow me to caress your pride

Until it stands at attention.

Give me permission to massage your mind

And if only for a moment,

Mold it to fit me perfectly.

Grant me passage to knead your tenderness

So that it merges well with my own.

Say it's okay that I gently kiss your grace

So that it never wants to leave.

Say I can nibble on your imagination

And make it sing a happy tune.

Come closer.

Let me experience you.

TK

Unpacking

Yeah, I've been MIA these past few days.

That's because I have been busy unpacking.

I have a lot of things to sort out in my heart and head

Before I can allow myself leisurely time again.

There are far too many boxes marked

"Triggers" and "Unresolved Issues" blocking my way

For me to go out and have a good time.

You and I have been doing that

"Maybe it'll take your mind off of it"

Thing for too long.

That's why I'm blocked in this corner now.

All of the boxes filled with

Depression, anxiety, fear and hurt feelings

Have left me with only a corner of myself to live in.

And I'm a house with an open floor plan.

So, you KNOW that's all wrong.

Right now, I can't even see down my own hallway,

Let alone see how to let you in.

Just give me a little more time to

Unpack and get things in order.

I'll see you again soon.

TK

Love

I write about you all the time. Those who don't know any better would think I knew you personally. Like a child holding on to some pipe dream of her favorite celebrity, I write scripts in my head of what I will say the day we meet. I dream that you will say you love my work and that someday we should collaborate. I watch as you move through the crowd sharing laughs and hugs with everyone you are more familiar with. My heart pounds as your fragrance fills the air. How I wish that just once, I could be the one on your arm. But here I am, writing scripts that will never play out. And you, my precious star, remain a dream far beyond my reach.

TK

Happily, Never After

Dear Cinderella,

There just aren't enough happy endings to go around. Some of our carriages really are just pumpkins and our fairy godmothers are just regular people with generous listening ears. No matter how much they love us, they will never have wands and they can never grant out hearts' desires. The regular rags we wear are all that remain when we look in the mirror. There will be no gowns or grand balls for us to attend. We don't get princes and our slippers are not made of glass. We have more than two wicked stepsisters and we are constantly on guard. At the end of our suffering, we don't get to live in castles. Nothing eases the pain or the memories of the loved ones we have lost. When we open our windows, we don't plan for the birds to know all the words to our songs. Nine times out of ten, they are just ditties we made up to get us through the day. We can sweep all we want, but everything is still dirty. We get nowhere. But we work so that we have purpose. We tell ourselves it will pay off. Watching you live and fall in love as you see the shiniest treasures of life allow those of us who weren't born to be princesses to have a glimmer of hope. At night, we tuck ourselves in with your tales and just hope they fill our dreams. We want to be convinced that we are worthy, if only for a moment.

Sincerely,

The Other Half

TK

Be Art

Give me goosebumps.

Make me tremble like the feel of a cool breeze over me.

Lie with me and watch my face light up when

Stevie sings.

Give me a joyous shout loud enough to match my own when I

Hear Prince growl.

Fly with me when I read Zora's words and

Follow the furl in my brow when

Maya speaks to me.

When Jean-Michel amazes me,

Return the air to my lungs.

Come with me when Carrie Mae and Gordon's pictures

Move me.

Sit next to me when I

Learn from Issa and Ava.

Join in on the grit and grime from Coogler.

Even if you aren't a poet,

Lay pretty and honest words on my ears

But don't be afraid to let the ugly truth slip through.

When I am all over the place,

Love the place I am all over.

Behold the artist in me.

Love me when I create.

Get inspired by me.

TK

Note: This is not my view of all men of the cloth. But those to which it applies...

After Church

Pastor, can I talk to you for a moment?
Your sermon got the saints fired up today.
You really did your job.
But on behalf of us who actually believe we are
Imperfect, I have a few questions.
You got a big response when you talked
About how young girls today need to prepare
Themselves to be the wives of tomorrow.
But Pastor, when will our husbands
Start their training?
When will the classes on cherishing your
Woman be taught?
And are we just gonna act like Sister Johnson
And Sister Williams don't have sons who
Have no clue they are brothers because
We're preserving Deacon Lawrence's name?
Wouldn't these young men or,
"Husbands of tomorrow" if you will,
Benefit from the example of a man who
Owned up to his transgressions?
And since many other future husbands
Are within earshot,
Shouldn't Deacon Evans stop eyeballing
Tiffany when she walks by and commenting
On how she's "built like a woman"?
I mean, she's only eleven.
From you, we always hear
"Seek and ye shall find".
So why is it frowned upon when I seek
Understanding by studying the Qur'an
In addition to my Bible?
I mean, essentially, they
Say the same things.
Is it really so bad that I would rather research
Than always take your word and keep
Staring at that picture of Kenny Loggins
In a robe before I bow my head in prayer?
His skin just doesn't look like bronzed clay to me.
That's all I'm saying.
But you, Sir, had plenty to say when LaShawn
Came to church with last night's club stamp
On her hand.

But no one said anything when
You stood in the pulpit with Sister Allen's
Lipstick on your collar.
Maybe I was the only one who saw that though.
You have had a long day, I know.
You probably want to go home and unwind,
Maybe throw back a few beers the way
You did during the incoherent phone calls
You made to me while I was away in college.
I appreciate you calling to check on me.
I just wish I could have understood you.
You said it was the devil's elixir for a reason.
I know you have to leave.
Speaking of which, that's a nice
New car you've got there.
It's good to see they are paying you well.
It must be because you take such good
Care of the Building Fund.
I'm just waiting to see the building you
MUST be building for us elsewhere.
It has to be spectacular because we have
Been contributing since I was ten and
This roof still leaks.
And I never found that verse in the Bible
That says all of my tattoos are bigger
Sins than your daughter's collection of
Baby daddies.
I'm sure it's in there because you imply it all the time.
But can you point it out?
And I'm sure you know where it says
That my mama's divorce is less holy
Than an eternity in a loveless marriage too.
Can you also show me where God said it was okay
That you and Sister Allen were together because you had
Moments of weakness and
He "ain't through with you yet"?
You don't have to show me now.
We can talk about it later since I know
You need to get to the track before they stop taking bets.
I had better take off this jacket before I
Go outside though.
I need to be prepared for all the
Fire and brimstone you'll send my way.
Have a good day, Pastor.
See you next Sunday.

TK

Not the Girl

I'm not the girl you fight for.

I'm not the one you regret losing and spend your whole

Life trying to get back.

I am not the girl who is responsible for the lonely tears

You cry at night.

I am not the girl who years after loving and losing me,

You just hope that another can measure up to.

I am the girl who loves faithfully and in spite of.

I am the girl who forgives and accepts apologies that have never

Actually been given.

I am the girl who wants to build a life with the one she loves.

I am that girl who speaks life into all you do.

I am the girl who wants to love you and only you

And do so perfectly.

I am that girl who knows the meaning of the word unconditionally.

I am not the girl you fight for because,

If you're smart, I'm the girl you should never want to lose in the first place.

TK

The Sorry You Didn't Say

I forgive you for loving me the way fools do.

You probably don't regret not seeing me just yet.

But I trust that someday you will.

You will think about the times I poured my heart out to you

And you never even bothered to follow the tide.

You will think about the times I said your name

And you couldn't hear the music in my voice.

You will think about the times I wrapped my arms around you

But you still turned cold.

You will pray for a random call from me in the middle of the day.

You will wish that you had given me everything.

You will look at all the wasted years

And calculate all the investments you should have made in us.

Their returns will astound you.

The days and nights when you are at your loneliest,

You will miss me.

But for now, I will just know that you're sorry

Or that if you aren't, you will be.

I give you my forgiveness.

And I give my aching heart its due rest.

TK

'Round Midnight

Usually 'round midnight,

I think of you.

Right in the center of my brain,

I build your universe.

I smirk at Fate

Because I am in on the secret.

I already know the joys

Of Me and My Thoughts

Being alone together.

TK

Ashes to Ashes: The Case for Cremation

When it is time for me to leave,
Please let me go.
Don't bury me in a vault in preparation
For visitors I cannot receive.
Do not make me and my shortcomings
Compost for the food that nourishes
The lives of others.
I don't want them to bear the aftertaste
Of my failures.
I don't want my doubts planted
In their souls.
I won't be sad that you have released me.
It will be my greatest joy.
I want you to let me fly in the wind.
My heart won't break because no one
Loves me.
For then, there will be hope of landing
Upon the cheek of someone who has
Known love.
I will mix with their tears of joy and
Finally know the taste.
I won't cry for the children I don't have.
Maybe then I can linger upon nursery
Windows and hear the gleeful
Little laughs I missed.
I won't think twice about how I have
Disappointed my friends and family.
Then I can wrap 'round roots of trees
And they can FINALLY see me grow.
I won't hurt for the beauty I don't have.
Then, I will greet the
Growing grass
The blowing wind
The rolling seas
The majestic thunder
The piercing lighting
The ever-present sky.
Do not cry for me.
Do not sit with a shell of me.
Do not let me stop your lives
When mine is done.
Instead, place me on the wind
And just let me go.

TK

Sentimental Mood

Sometimes the rain

Makes me feel sentimental.

But most of the time,

It just makes me feel…you.

TK

Zora

There is something in your gaze for me. There is a certain beauty to that cockiness in your smirk. It's a lesson in the power of always knowing something they don't. When I was ten, I learned your name. When I read your words, I looked around and no one understood you the way I did. I knew we were kindred spirits. Though I never saw the bony mule, there, I would find the best stories. You showed me how to hunt a story like a lioness, quiet and steady with a ferocious final pounce. When you told stories on the porch, I felt those experiences in my soul. I sat by you in The Sassy Susie as you tore down the streets. Through you, I saw the beauty in our people. When we laugh our big laughs and play the dozens, it is then that we sit closest to God. We use "ain't" and "y'all" even when we know better. And it is glorious. You were a Finer Woman long before I was born and long before I ever knew I wanted to be. Pretty early on, I had already taken your advice and started sharpening my oyster knife. You did it. So, I knew it was a good idea. I wanted to speak like you, walk like you and write like you. You were my guru. Hats tipped, long skirts, pants with high waists—you were equal parts grit and grace. Coming in with SPUUUUUUUUUUUUUNNNNNK and making sure everyone paid attention, you were all I needed to be. I say "needed" because you were the type of woman it would take decades for me to grow into. I watched my mother and grandmother closely the same way you did because I knew I would find a lot of my fodder there. Sometimes I wonder if you met my mother and whispered to her on that fall day that I was conceived. It seems you told her that on the day of the birth of Baldwin, she would bring forth a daughter who aspired to his uprightness and your tenacity and that the world would not be prepared. Like you, I didn't have a place, so I would have to make my own. I feel you every time I pick up a pen. I can see that smirk of yours when the thoughts start flowing. I want to write things that you would want to read. I want to pick up where you left of and tell the ugliest, most beautiful stories of us. I can only hope I make you proud.

TK

Forget Me Lots

Every day I have unwrapped your neglect.

I wish I could feign surprise at this point.

Your ribbons of rejection lay all around me

And there is nothing pretty about them.

Your bows of bypass perch all around me like shadows.

When you happen to remember me,

I do my best to muster up a note of excitement.

"Aw, you shouldn't have!"

Except, I mean you… really…. shouldn't have.

It would be more gracious of you to

Just ignore me all the time.

Then at least we won't have to pretend it is some

Grand gala when you make your presence known.

Just a thought.

TK

Be Free

I've never sought to cage a bird
That begged to be set free.
I respect its desires to be anywhere
Other than here with me.
Whether that bird be a lover
Or a once trusted friend,
I take heed to the fact that
Sometimes forever ends.
That bird should not be angry when I
Watch it fly away from me.
For I am doing as it has asked
And letting it be free.

TK

The Beautiful Struggle

"My art hurts." That's all I can say on days like this. These are the days when it hurts to create. I search for happy thoughts to write down. But I'm no fool. I don't believe a single one of them. I only attempt to close the door because I don't want my demons to get out. When they run rampant, they become difficult to wrangle and will destroy everything in their paths. And I would never wish that upon anyone. But for as much effort as I put up to control those feelings of sadness, fear and doubt, they bang loudly upon everything I am. When they knock, I use the sound to measure just how far I am from where I want to be. It's deafening. Rather than waste words, I usually just cry on paper. When I say it all out loud, it always seems to come out in another language and no one understands. When I speak, people give answers where there are no questions and ask questions for which there are no answers. So, I sit and write. I let my pain run free and I do not treat its rabidity. It grabs hold of my passion gnashes its teeth and engages in battle. Pain and Passion toss and tussle their way around my self-doubt. They fight and well up inside of me and I attempt to write out the hurt. I get cut, bruised and I bleed a lot. But I am lucky enough to always find beauty in the struggle.

TK

Functional

For you, I am Van Gogh's ear.

By that, I mean I may not be your entire story,

But I am the part that makes you intriguing.

While I may not be that one thing that makes you famous,

A lack of me would leave your story void.

You have had decades of eternities—

Things that drew themselves out

Seemingly just to spite you.

But the look in your eyes tells me that your forever—

That thing that never lasted but you wanted it to—

Didn't come before you kissed me.

I am all of your vices—

Those things that inflame you and give you purpose

But make you the least attractive to others.

I am that thing you can choose to live without

But my absence makes you the most imbalanced.

Like Frida's brow, I lead you from vision to vision.

My guidance, though bold and harsh,

Serves its purpose and enhances your beauty.

Regardless of ear or eyebrow,

I remain that one piece about the masterpiece

Of life that you so foolishly ignore.

TK

Up

Where are you right now?

Where is your mind?

These stars tell me your mind is on me.

But they probably lie.

All pretty things do.

We're written in them.

And because they loom over me as I sleep,

They're at the best angle to fill my head with happy things-

A kiss

A laugh

A touch

A life.

I don't know if these stars are lying or

Whether or not what we have is real.

But for now, I'll just stay here,

Blissfully looking up.

TK

Black People

I love the way we love each other.

The silence and mere nodding of heads as

We pass on the street says so much.

The prolonged games of Spades in the backyard

With the grill going

Frankie Beverly & Maze blasting

The chants of "Who made this?!"

Echoing through the kitchen

Nicknames like Canopy, Lil' Rich, Lil' Buddy

Dank, Popcorn, Goo-Goo and Peanut

That stick so well we forget given names

Learning to drive on Daddy's lap on long dirt roads

At the age of 6

Hardly putting on a pair of shoes for an entire summer

Sitting for hours and enduring the gripping of braids

That hurt a little for a moment but make our crowns more glorious

In the long run

Obligatory rounds of The Electric Slide at functions

And involuntary folding of the lips and wagging of the tongues

Complete with body rolls when our jam comes on

Skin ashy when fresh out of the tub

But shining like black gold after a touch of cocoa butter

Skin smooth, dark and usually looking

At least ten years younger than our chronological age

The way we walk and talk

The way we say "Nigga" knowing that we probably shouldn't

But feeling empowered when it comes from those who love us

Well-seasoned chicken

Hairstyles that defy gravity

Roots responsible for the birth of civilization

Grandmama's living room filled with cousins and play cousins

And a whole lot of love

Thick bottomed girls who grow more beautiful the more

They understand their ample assets

Men who carry themselves like royalty without a day of instruction

While holding the potential to do everything

The resilience to withstand a clutching of a purse when we enter elevators

Our faces being pressed against the hot hoods of police cars

And the intimidation we cause when we travel in groups

The power to show what we have created from hundreds of years of slavery

And using that same power to walk into any room knowing that our ancestors Are responsible for the creation of someone, something and possibly Everything in it

The way we say "Boo", "Baby" or "Suga" and make everyone want to

Emulate us

How we call a fellow Melanite we have never met "Bruh" or "Sis"

And it instantly feels like a family reunion

The way we are everywhere,

Everything

And we are always the vein—

I love that.

TK

The Other Woman

I've been asked if I hated her. Honestly, for a while, I did. But you know how they say hate is a wasted emotion? When I stopped hating her, I knew that to be true. I had allowed that hate for her to fill my head and heart so much that I no longer knew how to use all of me to prosper. I realized we were both dumb. We both believed his pretty words. But I pity her more than me. I knew him before he became that thing he couldn't recognize when he looked in the mirror. She touched his body when he belonged to someone else. I held his heart when it belonged only to me. I knew him in his purity when art and love fueled him. I knew him before he wore the mask of shame over his face. He wants to be in my life again because when you're unforgettable, they always come back. The Other Woman and I simply don't move in the same circles. We don't vibrate on the same frequency. Because of that, hating her really would be a waste. I learned from my pain. Her being The Other Woman and being left to hurt, grow and heal on my own is what showed me how utterly amazing I am.

TK

Ms. Cellophane

I've gotten really good at watching other
People fall in love.
I've gotten not looking jealous when I see that
Glimmer in their eyes down to a science.
I am so good at pretending I don't feel like my empty arms
Are useless when I see them hold each other.
I curl my lips into a smile each time I
See them kiss.
When I hear them say "I love you",
I pretend there's someone at home waiting to
Say it to me.
When they dance, I pretend I have never
Heard the song that plays
And I hang on every note until the end.
When I see them in pictures,
I focus on how green the grass looked
The day it was taken
Or I pretend to care where the people in the
Background are going.
When they exchange vows,
I pretend someday someone will say
Even prettier things to me.
The lovers watch me watch them.
I do it so well
That they never know that I'm there.

TK

Don't Give Up

Do you ever have those times in life when you are doing all you can and it seems nothing works? Well, My Dear, that is because you are not doing all you can. I say that not placing blame but letting you know from experience that those moments are designed to teach you that you are destined for greatness beyond your wildest dreams. There will be challenges and there will be tears. But know that it is okay to break so that you can build. I, for one, am already proud of you and cannot wait to see what you become. So, I beg of you, please don't give up.

TK

Liquidity

I love the way you flow through me.

Your voice is like hot lava through my mind.

Your words set fires with each syllable.

When you touch me, each finger is a ribbon of

Hot butter over my soul.

You drench me.

Your gaze covers me like hot wax and makes me

A cocoon of myself.

You make me see me.

You are the river that drowns me.

My lungs are full of you.

But you are that nectar that I thirst for.

You leave me wanting more.

Your strength carries me to great distances

Some of which I never knew existed.

Though I never know where I might end up,

I surrender and float away in you.

TK

Little One

I want you to have it all. I want you well-fed. I want your soul to never know that feeling of being hungry. I want you to never feel the need to be put into a box to feel closeness. I want all of you to run free. You will cry. But I want none of those tears to be because you feel I have left you. I am always open to you. I have no exact picture of what I want you to be. Even if I did, you would be too large to fit into it. I could never draw lines strong enough to hold your colors. Any frame I could craft would crack and splinter under the weight of your imagination. You are never wrong for your emotions but when they make you feel lost, I will help you chart the course. I am proud of you even in all the nothingness you do. When you simply stretch your limbs, I am proud that they spread farther than yesterday. When you express yourself, I am proud of your compassion. There are times I will be wrong. But I will allow you to be my teacher. I will give you what I have and be receptive to what you pour into me. I will never dim your light. Instead I will stand next to you with a matching pair of wide eyes at the wonder of how brightly that light can shine. I will carefully read every page of you and wait with bated breath for the next words you add to your story. And I will love you unconditionally with every pen stroke.

TK

STILL the Wrong Alice

I'm Alice. I always have been. But it seems I have always been the wrong one. First, I was wrong for my own Wonderland. Now I am wrong for yours. I've been here before. But I was hoping that if I left and decided to come back, things would be right. Things are different this time. You have built doors that I don't fit through and walls I am not tall enough to climb over. There are times they come down to meet me. But when they do, I am force-fed punishing pastries that disproportion me all over again. I look for answers everywhere. The caterpillar tells me from the beginning that his advice could be deadly. But like a fool, I listen anyway. He speaks and even though I choke on the smoke he blows, I crave his words. They are the salve for when you don't show up. I'm dying as we speak. But he makes me feel better too. The White Rabbit is late but he makes it clear that he is not coming to see me. He has plans with That Other Alice. The Right One. The one that is enough for you. The Door Mouse comes around, but I can tell she just does it to make me feel better. She pops up but offers no words, only a look of pity. There is no double talk from the Tweedles. There is just the heaviness of awkward silence because they are too polite to ask me to leave. The Cheshire Cat won't hang the moon for me. He smiles but his celestial acrobatics are for the one who deserves it. That Other Alice. The Right One. So here I sit with The Mad Hatter and The March Hare, a guest at a party that was thrown for someone else, praying for at least one impossible thing before breakfast.

TK

Mirror

You never know it

But we are always watching you.

We see you when you laugh.

We see you when you love.

We see you when you cry.

We have our eyes on you during your most intimate moments.

When you make love, we see you.

When you sleep, we watch.

We do it all for you.

It is because we watch you live

That you get to see yourselves.

We are the mirror you need and we

Show you your souls at every angle.

If not for us, you would never know that

Your face was beautiful.

You would never know that you have

The perfect stride

Or that the ride and size of your breasts are ideal

Or that the curls of your hair rhyme with heaven

Or that the hairs of your beard are similar

In softness to an angel's wings.

We show you how to apologize.

We show you how much better you look

When you love yourselves.

Without us, history would be lost

And civilizations would crumble.

We are writers.

We are painters.

We are photographers.

We are actors.

We are singer.

We are dancers.

We are instrumentalists.

We are voyeurs.

We are mirrors.

Every day, we introduce you to yourselves.

TK

Apparition

You meant a lot to me.

But to you, I was just another face.

Maybe not even that.

I was probably more of a whisper in the wind.

I allowed you to be a shaman.

You entranced me and summoned me

Only when it served you.

When I was ready to show you the deepest

Parts of me, you reminded me that I was

Just

A whisper...

In the wind.

I cried but you wouldn't have known.

After all, how many people pay attention

To whispers in wind?

Don't apologize.

I don't need it now.

On second thought, don't even bother to speak.

Soon, you will no longer exist to me.

It helps if you remain silent

The way ghosts of an abandoned past do.

TK

He Was Music

He did it, Girl.

He did exactly what I said I wouldn't let him do.

He…turned….me… on.

He gave me his bebop and his hip-hop

And said, "There you go, Baby. Do with that what you will."

Just as I was figuring out how to use it,

He stunned me with the buzz of his jazz.

He let his rimshots run red hot,

Flow over me and take

Control of my soul.

His syncopation sank in and his

Rhythm began to make my backbone slip,

My hips dip and my mind trip

And I didn't even know it.

He threw in his rock 'n roll and

Busted the eardrums of my inhibitions.

His feedback, I fed back to him in waves

Of admiration.

Then he put a country twang upon that thang

And made me wanna break up, make up and

Fall in love all over again.

He had me asking myself, "Girl, what are you doing?!"

I couldn't ignore the call of his classical

Movements of mayhem down my spine.

And the raw tone of his ska

Took me to heights unknown.

I said,

"Ahhhh. Sing to me, Papa di melody uh di Rasta

As we rewrite reggae, replant roots and regrow revolution.

Right about now, I'd follow you anywhere."

Oh, I'm sorry, Girl.

I was in my own world.

You just don't know how he made me feel.

Then he put it all together and threw it at me

Until I thought my head would explode.

My toes curled,

Eyes rolled back

And I lay paralyzed.

Then he laid me down and introduced me

To the parts of my neo-soul he has just enhanced.

He owned me.

He ravaged me.

And I liked it.

TK

rEVOLution

I want to love myself in a way that no one ever has. I want it to be one of those things that is so divine that even *I* feel like there must be a catch. When I wake, I want to feel so good that I side eye myself. When I lie down, I want to feel every fiber of the sheets on my skin and to vibrate from the inside out just off the basis of my own energy. I want to have to ask myself "What do you want from me?" Even though, I know the answer will be "Just be you in a way that is more magnificent than yesterday", I still want to stay in touch that way. I want to stand up and show up for myself even when no one else does. I want to face battles and go against the grain for myself. I want to never feel the need to compare myself to others and to always protect myself from that pain. I want to love myself freely and openly. I want to love myself despite everything. I want it to change the way I live. I want self-love that feels like revolution.

TK

How to Love

Wayne said it.

I've had a lot of crooks try to steal my heart.

I've never really had luck,

Couldn't ever figure out how to love.

But it was supposed to be different for us. We were enrolled in those same classes. We were supposed to take the same tests along the way and work together to learn all the same lessons in love in the end. But I was the only one who showed up to class every day. You hit that chapter you couldn't understand. But instead of coming to me and asking for the notes, you let pride take over. And you failed.

You became one of my moments that didn't last forever.
You left me in that corner trying to put it together.
A lot of our dreams transformed to visions.
I had to learn they weren't mistakes but piss poor decisions …about love.

You might not have had a lot of crooks try to steal your heart.
But wanting to love honestly is just how that shit starts.
THEN how do you love?
How do you love?
I'm here in this moment I hope won't last forever.
I'm spending all my time trying to put me back together.
I wanna love.
I just wanna love.

TK

Nope

I won't allow you to inspire me. I won't give you the satisfaction of allowing me to feel that same tingle in my mind that I feel all over my body when I say your name. I won't allow you to become every drop of ink from my pen and display your precious ebony to put it all to shame. I'm not gonna let your voice echo in my head and narrate every moment of pleasure. I won't acknowledge the way you have impaled my insecurities and decapitated the darkness within me and even made me smile a little bit. I am not discussing how I probably bobbed when I should have weaved because these feelings keep knocking me the hell out. I'm not gonna tell you why I'm blushing. Don't worry about why I feel so good. We're not having that discussion. So, let's just move on.

TK

Dazed & Confused (Thinking In My Garage)

I don't know what I'm doing.
For years, I thought I did but that's all out the window now.
My heart was that thing I used to give the rest of me the stamina to chase after love.
I always thought my heart was pretty impressive
So, I ran with it in my hands screaming "Look at this!"
Until I was out of breath.
I would always run.
I never felt like anyone else had to run like I did.
But I thought my heart was just different that way.
I saw it as this athlete that was just *supposed* to run.
I would rest it, but I never gave it proper therapy.
I would take it in my hands again and just restart the race.
But now I'm confused.
I was giving my heart the rest it needed when you happened by.
You had seen me running before.
But I guess I had gotten so good at it that you didn't even notice I was doing it.
There were times you were out of breath trying to catch up.
Still, we had great conversations.
Even though I still had that same old heart I had been using and
Pushing to the limit, you stayed.
Eventually, I noticed I wasn't screaming anymore.
Instead, I was calmly saying "See me"
And you replied, "I always have".
So, here I am, loving openly,
Dazed and confused.
I have all this vulnerability that I never wanted and don't know what to do with.
I'm this person who feels pain at the thought of it all ending.
I am this person who gets excited when I hear from you and notices when I don't.
I'm tasting that sweet and sour flavor of my heart being idle
After falling over hurdles
But thinking it can still get up and win all by itself.
It has never been okay with having too much help.
I'm here.
With all of me engaged.
Lost.
And hoping you are just as confused as I am.

TK

Anachronistic

I am a love song, but I assure you I'm not one of those new tunes.

I don't contain incantations that will make you open

Your legs before you open your heart.

Nah. I'm not one of those.

I'm a timeless tune that repeatedly gives you the thrill

Of running to catch up with your runaway heart.

And I don't do that digital stuff.

I play on that old phonograph you have never wanted to get rid of.

I play you what is raw so that you can learn

To love all the static in my background.

There is no grinding to my melody.

When I play, you sweep your lover into your arms and

Wish I would never end.

I am sweet and gentle, but there is sorrow in me.

That sorrow is because they don't write them like me anymore.

I always play solo.

But I play boldly because it is the only way I know.

Through every window, I make myself known—

Never out of sync, but forever out of time.

TK

Home

I came home today and only you were here.
You're always here.
But today was different.
Usually you sit off somewhere in a corner.
You aren't usually the focal point.
I can usually look at the pieces of me that lie on my couch
When I should really be gathering them and
Placing them neatly on my therapist's couch to allow
Them to be properly deconstructed.
I can usually get distracted by the light from the face
Of my cell phone when I get a call from that man
Who is no good for me.
Then my focus shifts to the pitter patter of my heart
That I never noticed until that moment because
After all, nothing ever happened for me until it happened
On his time.
I can usually distract myself by agonizing over the stories
I have been given that I don't always recognize as gifts
Because how dare I have the audacity to write them?
I can usually keep myself busy sending birthday texts
And doing welfare checks on people who never think of me.
On those calls, I can focus on not letting my insides
Scream out loud.
I can usually look at all of my clothes and complain
That I have nothing to wear
When the real problem is, I really long for someone
I can be safely naked with.
I have spent a lot of time pushing those things aside.
I pushed and pulled them so far into corners
That they ended up on the lawn.
Today, Myself, I came home to just you.
I've lived with you before.
But now that it's just us, I want to learn to love you too.

TK

Black

Black is the absence of color.
But my Black doesn't fit that definition.
See, **MY** Black is more of the "absorption of all light" sort.
That means **MY** Black holds everything
And it doesn't need what you have to be beautiful.
MY Black is what you see when you turn off the lights.
It stops you in your tracks and makes you think hard
About your next move.
MY Black is the night.
It is the cloak of comfort that drapes over you after
A hard day's work.
MY Black is essential.
It goes with everything.
MY Black is oil and coal.
It fuels everything you have.
You might say **MY** Black is the absence of color.
But that makes it the reference point that taught you what
Colors were in the first place.
The black you know might be the absence of light,
A stain
Or a bruise.
But you can keep that black for yourself.
I don't need it.
It isn't mine.

TK

Lear

I want to leave the way King Lear did—

Silently and without commotion.

When my "She dies" is written,

There will be no need for overt pomp and circumstance Because there will have been an abundance throughout my life. I will leave my kingdom to my daughters without contest

But my Cordelias will be my favorites.

I will not banish them for their defiance.

They will have found no need to compete

For my affection and know that nothing they could ever say Would rival the love I felt as I walked beside them.

My Cordelias—my strong, reflective, silent, genuine types— Will be the perfect queens.

In my fifth and final act,

There might be tears.

But I want the tears to weaken against the

Joy in a smile I have given

The peace in the words I have written

The comfort in a kiss I have left.

I want no prolonged grief but the celebration of

My life and my example.

I want it all to be said and done at

"She dies."

TK

www.ingramcontent.com/pod-product-compliance
Lightning Source LLC
Chambersburg PA
CBHW061749290426
44108CB00028B/2938